CHASE EZIO

SELLING ON AMAZON

The Essential Guide to Amazon Sales Secrets, Learn About Effective Techniques and Strategies to Achieve Selling Success on Amazon

Descrierea CIP a Bibliotecii Naţionale a României
CHASE EZIO
   SELLING ON AMAZON. The Essential Guide to Amazon Sales Secrets, Learn About Effective Techniques and Strategies to Achieve Selling Success on Amazon / Chase Ezio – Bucharest: Editura My Ebook, 2021
   ISBN

CHASE EZIO

SELLING ON AMAZON

The Essential Guide to Amazon Sales Secrets, Learn About Effective Techniques and Strategies to Achieve Selling Success on Amazon

My Ebook Publishing House
Bucharest, 2021

CONTENTS

Getting Started Making Money
With Amazon – Part 1

Since you're here reading this, you've likely already heard about how you can make money with Amazon Affiliate Program. Perhaps you have already created your own website and hosted it in hopes of making some good coin with Amazon Affiliate Program. If you are unsure exactly how to do that, you aren't alone. Here are some steps to get you started.

1. *Learn basic HTML* – If you don't know HTML already, now is a good time to learn it. It will help to keep your costs down and give you more flexibility. Many sites are WYSIWYG but the trouble is you lack any flexibility when it comes to creating hyperlinks, formatting text, and carrying out other tasks that can help you to make money with Amazon. There are tons of HTML tutorials online so in no time at all you can learn the basics.

2. *It's time to decide what your niche or topic will be* – If you are planning to make recommendations, do product reviews, or just talk about a certain product or products in an effort of selling that product. Make sure you choose a narrow niche that is distinct and will be easy to target. For example Latin dance, card making, Jack Russell, etc.

3. *Pick the domain name* – make sure that you give this the thought it deserves. Choose a name that is keyword rich to help you with SEO, a name that is relevant, and matches your niche. Of course, it will have to be available so have a few options that you'll be happy with.

For example, latindanceforbeginners.com easycardmaking.com or ilovejackrussel.com you can also be creative in case the domain you want isn't available by using hyphens, such as latin-dance- for-beginners.com or choose a different domain extension. There are tons – for example net, ca, org, edu, etc.

4. *Register the domain name* – Many hosting sites are set up so you can register your domain right away but if not you can register it separately through many different sites. Once you register your domain name, it will be yours to use. Registering a domain for a year ranges from $10 to $20 on average.

5. *Setup web hosting* – This is where you need to be careful. There is really expensive web hosting and generally there is no reason to pay high rates. Even if they offer all kinds of tools most people don't use the majority of these features and you'll be paying for them. You should be able to find hosting for as little as $5 a month, and for as little as $10 you can find hosting for unlimited sites.

There you've got a good start. Read Part 2 for the final steps in getting started making money with Amazon.

Getting Started Making Money
With Amazon - Part 2

In Getting Started Making Money With Amazon Part 1, we walked through the steps up until finding your web hosting. Now let's look at the final steps to getting started.

1. *Install the blog software* – Why blog software? Because it will provide with the necessary structure to make it easy for you to run an effective site and post new content easily. WordPress is the most popular. It is open source, which means it's free, it's easy to install, and it is extremely powerful. Many web hosts have a one-step process for installation, or just download and follow the instructions provided.

2. *Make it look good* – One of the perks to WordPress is all the templates that you have to choose from. In addition to the hundreds of free themes, there are hundreds of WordPress

themes you can buy. Pick a theme that looks good, ties to your niche, has the layout you want, and offers what you want to be able to do in terms of tools.

3. *Create your categories* – Your blog software should allow you to setup categories that help you to organize your entries so it is easier for your visitors to find what it is they are interested in reading. For example, your Jack Russel site might have a number of categories such as training, eating, toys, etc.

4. *Become an Amazon Associate* – The sign up is simple, and it's free. Just go to the Amazon site and at the bottom click the 'Join Associates' link. You'll want to have your site set up – at least the basics with some content, as they are going to review your site.

5. *Create the blog posting links* – There are different ways to create your links. You can use the tools offered by your blog software, but the easiest way is using the Amazon Build A Link tool. Log into your Associate page, and find the product you want to review. Build your personalized link. There are a number of options for link building but most would tell you that the text links are most effective.

6. *It's time to blog* – The time has come to write your blog review and post it. You will insert your link code to the product on the Amazon site (created above) that you are writing the review for. You will want to include a number of reviews.

7. *Promote your website* – Make sure you take time to promote your website/blog. There are all kinds of online communities that can help you do this, as well as social media, directories, etc. The more exposure the better!

There you have it – in Part 2 we have set you up so that you are ready to start making money with your Amazon affiliate program. So what are you waiting for? Why not get busy today?

Can You Make Money With
the Amazon Affiliate Program?

If you have been looking at the Amazon affiliate program and wondering if it is right for you, the only person that can answer that question is you. But we are going to provide you with all kinds of reasons why you should consider this program.

#1 Commissions

Many don't think the 4% commission is adequate, but consider the difference it makes between a $10 disk, which is .40 cents, and a $5000 camera, which is $200 – suddenly the 4% doesn't seem all that bad. In addition, it's pretty easy to take the 4% to 6%. All you need to do is sell seven items. Now consider this – if you make your seven items, using low ticket items that sell fast, that puts you in place for the high ticket items at a higher price. You have make as much as 8.50 percent when you reach the higher end of the selling scale.

#2 People Purchase More Than a Single Item

One thing that is great about Amazon is that it is like 'one stop shopping.' You send them to the site – they buy 'your' advertised item and then they shop some more – you get paid. Or if they leave the site but come back within 24 hours you still get your commission. So let's look at an example. You send a potential customer to the site because they are going to buy a 'book' you promoted. When they get there they not only find buy the book they buy a headset, and then finish their purchase with a new phone. Now you'll get paid commission on all of those items.

#3 Remember That Every Little Bit Adds Up

Initially the commissions may seem small. You may think how can you possibly earn a living with small commissions – after all 4% on a $10 item is .40 cents. Celebrate these little payouts because before long one item is ten items and ten items is a thousand items. Before long to go with the ten dollar items are the items that cost hundreds of dollars. Soon your

14

commission checks will grow and you will enjoy the benefits of a steady income. So be patient. Make sure that you provide plenty of links on your website or blog to bring people to the products you are selling.

#4 Many Links to Products

As we touched on above, make sure that you are providing many links to the products you want your site visitors to click and eventually purchase. The more links the more likely that you will have a sale complete. Don't be afraid to place your links strategically in your content or article.

Why Amazon Affiliate Program
is Better Than Others

Whether you are new to affiliate marketing or been around for some time. If you find yourself struggling, you have just landed at the right place, because by the time you are finished reading this article, you will be ready to maximize your income with the right affiliate program. It is time you learned why Amazon Affiliate Program is better than the others.

The first thing you need to understand is that there is no such thing as success as an online marketer through luck. It doesn't just happen for some and not happen for others. It comes from hard work and understanding what makes it work, and Amazon Affiliate Program is certainly one that is worth understanding. Why Amazon Affiliate better than others?

1. *You do not need to pre-sell*. There is a lot less skepticism from your visitors when they are looking at buying

physical products over digital products. That's because with digital products you really don't know what you are getting until after you make the purchase, where as with physical products you know what it is you are buying in all aspects. Physical goods are also more popular because the product is tangible – you can feel it, touch it, see it, and hear it. It will stimulate all four of your senses in a way digital products can't.

2. *There is zero saturation.* You've probably heard the stories yourself about products that are 'over sold online' to a group that is marketed to, such as with how to make money programs. When you are selling Amazon products, you do not have to ever worry about too much competition because it does not exist. Tens of thousands of a single product can be sold every year, and you do not have to be concerned with any one marketer cornering the market.

3. *You do not have to do a lot of selling yourself.* Most of the Amazon products sell themselves. You do not have to work hard at selling like you do with digital products. For example, you don't need a sales page and you don't need to become best buds with all the top marketers.

There you have it - three excellent reasons why Amazon Affiliate Program is better than many of the others on the market. Amazon provides you with an opportunity to build yourself an excellent income source with reputable products that are readily available.

Significantly Increase Amazon Affiliate Sales
Using a Best Seller List

Many people have turned to the Amazon Affiliate program because of the potential revenue opportunity it offers. However, just a many do not understand how they can significantly increase their Amazon affiliate sales and increase their commissions exponentially. That well kept secret is the 'Best Seller List.'

The actual technique isn't new. Many businesses will create a 'Best Seller List.' The music industry and book industry have been doing it for decades. Amazon does it too! Feel free to think outside the box here and create your own Best Seller list. This list can be posted on your blog, in your articles, or among your content on your website.

Why Best Seller Lists Work Well

Your bestseller list should contain 6 to 10 products in your category. You can have one or more categories.

* Consumers love to be part of trends. They hate being left out.

* We claim we are unique individuals, but the truth is we are social creatures and we want to know what others are doing.

* We are by nature lazy and so we love short cuts to find something that appeals to us.

* There's a certain kind of wisdom that occurs in crowds. We like to see what's happening in the crowd.

Results of Your Best Seller List

There are several results you can enjoy from your bestseller list.

* *Sales* – Each time you produce a list you should see an increase in your sales on Amazon. Of course, that's assuming the list links to the item on Amazon.

* *Conversion* – While conversion rates vary, you should enjoy a conversion rate that was higher than prior to your list creation.

* *More Commission* – A higher conversion rate means more sales, and more sales mean more commission owed to you. And it potentially has the ability to increase your commission rate from 4% to 6% since you are required to only sell 7 items for the jump to occur.

How to Increase your List Longevity

This is an effective technique but you want to get the maximum time out of your list. You don't want to have to be changing your list weekly as this requires time. A better option is to choose items for your list that will stay popular at least for a 4 week period. Some items will have even a longer shelf life. Take advantage of it!

Tricks to Making Money through
Amazon Affiliate Program

Amazon Affiliates has provided many entrepreneurs with a comfortable income. But not everyone has been successful, so we thought now would be a good time to share a few tricks that have helped others be successful.

If you want to boost your payout on high priced products sell larger quantities of those inexpensive products. Expensive items over a $100 are what you really want but to boost the commission rate you can include those lower priced items because these are easier to sell. You can have different websites set up for each niche so that they don't cross paths on the same site. Higher priced items are sold less frequently but you only have to sell seven items to raise your commission rate from 4 percent to 6 percent, so if you sell seven small items, which is easier, you can enjoy a higher commission on your larger ticket items.

Make sure that you use multiple tracking ID's for each of your sites. Amazon's default is to assign you one tracking ID, but you can create up to one hundred tracking ID's. And if you create that many you just have to ask for more so don't be afraid to create these tracking IDs so you can see what's going on. After all, you would not use the same Google Analytics code on all your websites would you? So why would you do it with Amazon. You need to see where your traffic is coming from along with what products they are driven to in order to be able to make sound buying decisions.

Make sure that you create a product comparison grid for each of the products that you are marketing within your niche. Then allow your visitors to sort by the different features of each of the products. This is an excellent way to increase your sales. In fact, it can generate as much as 10 percent more income for you. It is a tool that is often overlooked, but it has so much potential.

Add a 'buy it now' button to your content or articles and make it convenient for people to buy your items. In fact, it has been shown that you can increase your income by as much as 10% by adding a simple buy button. That's definitely worth the little time it takes to create and insert the button on your sites.

There you have it – just a few tricks that you can put to use on your website or blog to increase your Amazon income.

Tips to Amazon Affiliate Program Success

Amazon Affiliate Program offers the potential to earn significant revenue. The more tips and tricks you have the more you'll be able to earn. Let's have a look at these tips to enjoying Amazon Affiliate Program Success.

#1 Music is a better choice than books or other products in this category. Why? Because your visitor can listen to short clips off the album (about 10-15 minutes worth) and get really hooked on the music, which leads to them buying the album. There are very few consumer goods that you can try before you buy, but music is one of them and that leads to a higher sales rate than other categories. Remember you only need to sell seven items to increase your commission from 4% to 6%.

#2 You need to learn some HTML – don't worry you just need to learn the basics – it's not too hard. Otherwise you will have to rely on purchased software that does the coding for you or software offered on the site (such as WordPress), and you will not get exactly what you want. Plus many of these software WYSIWYG programs are code heavy and the search engines do not like this.

#3 If you want to know all the details about your visitors so that you can improve your conversion rate, you should sign up for Google Adsense. The sign up is free and it will help you to determine what's working and what's not. It will help you make all kinds of decisions about what you should do on your blog or website.

#4 You should always set earning expectations that are reasonable, especially when you are starting out. Every business takes time to grow, and online businesses such as your Amazon Affiliate Program are no different. Remember, you'll get paid for sales that occur within a 24- hour period, so even when a customer doesn't buy immediately there's still a chance you'll earn. You'll also get paid a commission if your lead buys more than just the click through item and that's a great way to increase your profits.

Amazon Affiliate Program offers something that many other affiliates don't and that is the wide range of products that you can be paid on. Even though your visitor clicks through and buys Widget A if they buy other items on the Amazon site, no matter what they are, you will be paid on those items too. It's common for a person to buy multiple items.

Amazon offers an opportunity for a steady income stream. These tips will help you to be successful.

Amazon Affiliate Program Integrates With Blogger

Amazon Associates has integrated their affiliate program with Blooger, which will make it easier for bloggers to add relevant Amazon product links to their blog posts without having to interrupt the editing process on their blogs. Amazon Associates for Blogger can be found on your Associates Central web page. You will want to take advantage of this.

Sign up is quick and easy. Assuming you already have an Amazon Associate account, you can use your Associate ID. If you are new you can have your Associate ID almost instantly. For existing associates it will only take you a couple of minutes to sign up, and you will instantly have access. You will be able to turn the Amazon Product Finder on or off depending on your preference.

The new tool makes it simple to add Amazon links to your blog posts, either text or image links. There are just two steps. First type and highlight the text in your blog post that's relevant.

The Amazon Product Finder will search through the millions of products on the Amazon site and recommend those it feels are a close match with the text you highlighted. Then you can insert an image or link to that product, which will include your ID. If you are using a blog editor you might find it easier to write your entire post in the program and then post the draft on Blogger and then use the Amazon product finder.

By signing up for Amazon Associates for Blogger you will also be able to add dynamic content in the sidebar of your blog using the new sidebar gadgets that are being provided. The Amazon Deals gadget and Amazon Search box are excellent tools to help your visitors find exactly what they are looking for. If you want to add these to the sidebar just got to 'Add a Gadget,' and then type in Amazon to find the gadgets you want.

If there is a disadvantage to adding the gadgets to the sidebar it is that it can slow down page load times. You will have to experiment and decide for yourself whether the load times are acceptable.

The new Amazon Associates Blogger tools are going to make it a great deal handier to get your links in place and start to enjoy earning revenue. Don't be discouraged if things start slow. It can take a bit of time to create a blogging environment that consistently makes money for you, but don't give up.

The Golden Rule to Making Money
with Amazon Associate Program

If you are just getting started using Amazon Associate Program before you jump in promoting products, there is something you should know – The Golden Rule – actually there are a handful of golden rules you should follow that will help you make money with Amazon.

#1 The products you choose should always be over $100.

Because Amazon's commission is only 4% for the item that sells, it's important to sell higher priced items if at all possible. That percentage can go as high as 8.25% if you sell sufficient product quantities. You will make more money when high priced products sell, compared to low priced products. Amazon allows you to sort by price making it easier to find the products you want to sell.

#2 The products you choose should get a minimum of a 4 star review.

For success, it is key for you to promote products that have good reviews. You will get a much higher conversion rate on products that have a good review. These days' people like to do a lot of research before they decide what they will buy. After all, it's easy with the internet to review products and find the best products. Therefore, if you are promoting products that have a low review score people simply are not going to buy them because they know that there are better options.

#3 Always create a blog that's like a review with only the best content and use text links, which Amazon readers prefer over widgets.

If you ask bloggers who are successful with Amazon earnings they will tell you that they do best when they do product reviews. That's because people like to read reviews before they make their choice. The more compelling your review the faster you will make Amazon income. It's really that simple.

To start your review blogging you do not even need your own domain name and you don't have to purchase hosting. You can start by using one of the blogging sites that host blogs. The one thing that you should do is choose your name (Subdomain) to be close to the product name. For example, if you are promoting XYZ Treadmills then choosing a name like XYZ-treadmills would be wise. This helps with your search engine optimization and that's important for potential customers to find you, because it is what will help you rank well in the search engines.

The Secret to Increase
Your Amazon Associate Income

If your goal is to make income through affiliate programs, one of the programs you will want to investigate is the Amazon Associate Program – this one is certainly worthwhile to have a look at. There are tons of affiliate programs out there, but not all of them are created equal. In fact, many don't really generate a great deal of income, but Amazon Associate Program is different.

Amazon affiliate program makes it easy to drop your HTML code in your blog, articles, or content. You make your selection for what you would like to see on your page and Amazon gives you the code – you just cut and paste. It has been proven that the text links do best. What's nice about these is that you can actually change the text to fit your article, blog, or content.

Amazon Associate Program has plenty of options even if you are just starting out. The 4% commission might not seem to appealing but there's plenty of potential here because when just seven items are sold that commission jumps to 6%. Let's have a look at the secret to increasing your income on Amazon.

You are going to want to find your niche and then search engine optimize your pages for the product you are going to sell. For example, let's say you are going to focus on toasters. Then you will want to SEO your page to bring targeted traffic to your site.

You want to focus on the bigger ticket items for your main commission because 4% of $100 is much better than 4% of $10, so at least some of the items you are going to market needs to be higher ticket. Don't be afraid to include thousand dollar items as well.

However, there's a little trick that can help you increase your commission percentage and your overall income. We already mentioned to get to the 6% commission rate you only have to sell seven items a month. You also already know that smaller ticket items always sell faster. So set yourself up so that you can move tons of these small products easily. That will instantly bump your commission up so that you are making more on those big ticket items.

There is a higher rate of 8.5% but that one's a little tougher to reach, as you have to sell thousands of items, so focus on the 6% at least in the beginning.

Amazon offers you a wide array of products, so many that no matter what your niche is you should have no problem finding a product to promote and sell. So make the most of what Amazon can give you – The Amazon Associate Program has a lot to offer in income.

Tips and Tricks
to Generate Amazon Income

Earning revenue through the Amazon affiliate program offers a great deal of potential to anyone who takes the time to really figure out how to really get the most out of it. Let's look at just a few tips and tricks that can increase your revenue.

One trick that works well for many is to find a way to publish recurring deals. If you can frequently mention products on sale it can increase your revenue, and an easy way to do this is just to post weekly deals. You can include this in your content and make it appear in a way that your visitor feels you are offering them valuable information. If you have the time, you can do it as a daily deal posting each day instead of weekly.

You can also publish a monthly list of bestsellers. These might not always be in your niche. It's a bit like a trending list, in fact, you could call it that if you like. You can find out what the bestsellers are on Amazon just by going to www.amazon.com/bestsellers. If you want more visitors and more exposure than write an article that talks about one or more of these bestselling products. It's a good idea not to make your list include more than 10 bestsellers or it will lose its effectiveness.

Carousel banner ads have proven to work better than the static banner ads. The carousel widgets are interactive and will generally display about a dozen products in the banner. It is easy to create an Amazon carousel banner right in your associate account. You can even add products manually if you want to or just display those that are bestselling.

Don't waste your time creating an Amazon Astore. Many find the conversion rate is awful – less than 1 percent of total sales. If you aren't convinced you can try it for yourself, but many of the high earners don't bother wasting their time here.

You'll do better just getting the people over to Amazon.com through your text links. You can expect this to be your main focus for revenue generating. When you send someone to Amazon and they buy within 24 hours of initially going there, you'll get paid your commission. And if the customer ads it to the cart but doesn't complete, if they go back and buy within 30 days, you will get your commission. This is the most effective way to make money with your Amazon affiliate program.

It is possible to earn a full time income through Amazon. These tips and tricks are a good start.

Make Money With Amazon and Your Blog

Are you looking to make some money with your blog? When you start blogging and your focus is to make some money, it can be a bit daunting finding revenue sources. One of the quickest and easiest is to open up an Amazon Associate account.

Once you open your Amazon account, you can sprinkle your articles with Amazon HTML links, which are based on the products you choose to promote on your blog. These custom links send those that click to the item on Amazon's page, and if they purchase the product, you are paid a commission. What's nice is that these links are on your blog forever, and that means you can be paid commissions for an endless period of time.

Signing up for your Amazon account is pretty easy. Look at your analytics to determine where your traffic is coming from. For most people The US Associates account is the best choice as it allows you to appeal to the most people, but if you focus on a product that targets let's say a British market, then you would want a British Associate signup.

Once your account is set up, you'll place links in your blog, which is pretty straight forward. You'll log into your Amazon account and you'll find the product that you want to link to. All you need to do is click 'Link to this page,' and simply follow the instructions that are given to you, which will be based on how you want your link to look. The text option is the most popular because it also gives you flexibility to change the text but that's up to you. Don't be afraid to experiment, especially in the early times to find what works for you. Then you'll simply take the HTML code that is given to you and place it in your blog.

Generally, the more you sell the more commission you'll make. General product commissions start at 4%, but after just six sales in a month that increases to 6%. Then there are incremental increases of .5% all the way up to 8.5%. Remember, this applies to general products. Many specialty categories like electrical goods remain at 4% no matter how many units you sell. Then again, some categories like digital goods are set at 10%, while others have a cap. Be sure to read on Amazon, so as not to be surprised.

It doesn't take long to start to make money. It's quicker than you might think. Things like

'Favorite Picks' or 'Top 10 Lists' can really begin to generate income quickly. Don't be afraid to experiment! There are bloggers that make a full time income from selling Amazon products on their blogs. You can too!

5 Tips for Using Amazon Affiliate Program on Your Blog

Amazon Affiliate Program has become increasingly popular because of the income potential it offers. Let's look at 5 tips for using Amazon Affiliate Program to get the best results from your blog.

1. Think About Who Your Audience Is

It's a good idea to think about who your audience is – put yourself in your reader's shoes – what are they looking for when they surf your blog. If you look at things through your readers eyes you will do a much better job of targeting your traffic.

2. Personal Endorsement

Personal endorsement is an excellent tool for generating a high click through rate. You see just adding links randomly throughout your blog may not be enough to generate that click. What will generate that trust is trust, when a visitor returns day after day and builds an online relationship with you. In fact, if you want to destroy all your hard work, just recommend they buy something you don't really believe in. If you want to increase your click through and your conversion, rates talk about the pros and cons of products. People like to hear the good and the bad so they can make their own decisions. If you do this, and then endorse products you believe in you will see a real change in your commission checks.

3. Link to Top Notch Products

Choose companies and products that are reputable to share links with. Nothing will send someone away from your blog never to return, than proving links to poor quality products.

4. Deep Links Work Best

Many think all they have to do is put a banner across the top and people will make their way to Amazon and you'll make some money. Actually, that's not true at all. What does work is placing deep links within your content. It is more work but it also pays more and that's your goal.

5. Consider Link Placement

There are some hotspots on every page – left hand side bar, end of the post, or inside the content. Make sure that's where you place your links to get the highest click through rate.

The days of any affiliate program making you money without some work are pretty much gone. But it doesn't have to be hard or complicated. These 5 tips are a great start to making your Amazon Affiliate Program work.

5 Mistakes Amazon Affiliate Marketers Make

Amazon Affiliate Program has a lot to offer marketers, yet you will still hear about those who don't enjoy the success of revenue earnings worth talking about. Let's look at 5 mistake Amazon affiliate marketers make that can drastically reduce your income.

1. **Too many products** – it's a common mistake beginners make. They market too many products. Yes, you need to build multiple streams of income through different products, but the trouble is you can spread yourself so thin that you cannot properly manage all the streams you are attempting to create and maintain, and that sets you up for failure. Choose your products carefully making sure they fit your niche.

2. **Not testing** – Nothing will break the trust of your visitors faster than being lead to a product that is junk or doesn't work in the way you claim it does or the manufacturer claims it does. Before you promote a product make sure you have either personally tested the product or done your research to see what others think of it.

3. **Not tracking** – It is important that you assign a unique tracking affiliate link on each page you promote a product so that you an later determine where the sale came from. By doing this you can determine which pages are nicely converting so that you can grow your business. It is easy to create a unique tracking ID with Amazon. Just log into your Amazon Affiliate dashboard, then click on 'account settings' (top right), then click on 'manage tracking IDs.' Now you can create a new tracking ID that will allow you to track the web page and/or campaign the item is sold from.

4. **Not comparing** – One of the best ways to convert visitors to buyers is by using the comparison technique. When buyers are ready to buy, they tend to narrow their options down to 2-3 choices. If you create a 3 Best (Insert Product) for (Insert Use) you are in a position to help your visitor finalize their

decision. Comparison websites are profitable so keep this in mind.

5. **Not helping** – One of the biggest mistakes marketers make is to spend their time trying to sell rather than trying to help your visitors. Avoid those annoying phrases like "BUY NOW," or "BUY RIGHT NOW," screaming at your visitor in capital lettering. Instead, take the time to help your visitor learn about the product(s). Why do you think Amazon products do so well – those reviews are extremely powerful? People respond much better to the helper sales person rather than the shark sales person.

How to Use Article Marketing
to Increase Amazon Revenue

The Amazon Affiliate Program provides an excellent opportunity to build a steady revenue source. There are a number of ways to incorporate Amazon products into your site, but one method that works very well is to include your Amazon product or products in articles. Here are the steps to do just that.

1. First you will need to login to your Amazon Affiliate Program at amazon.com using your username and your password, which was provided to you upon signup.

2. Once you have logged in you need t go to the best selling products, which you can select from the drop down list. Then choose the product type you want to sell.

3. After you select the product, you need to click on the get link to copy your affiliate link. Amazon has made this a very easy process for you.

4. Now copy and paste the link into your document. You will insert it shortly.

5. Start the process of writing your recommendation. Make sure that you provide detail. Talk about the good and that bad, the pros and the cons. Make your article between 300 and 500 words. Don't go much over 500 words because you will lose your reader – their attention span is simply not that long.

6. Now it is time to put your article on the web for others to read. There are a number of article banks out there, but Ezine Articles, which is found at http://www.ezineartlces.com is one of the most popular and recommended. If you do not yet have an account here, or at any of the other article banks, you wish to use, then you need to create an account. You will need to provide your information and a photo so your customers can feel like they know a little about you.

7. Paste your article and then in the signature line at your Amazon Affiliate URL, which you obtained earlier.

8. If you have another product then repeat the steps again.

If you don't like to write or you are not a good freelance writer there are many sites online where you can hire a qualified writer to write your article for you. This is an excellent way to ensure you get a top quality article. You can also use freelance writers to write your content for your site too.

Amazon Affiliate Program offers you an excellent opportunity to earn income and with a little work, you can turn this into a full time income opportunity.

5 Great Tips to Earning Income
With Amazon

Amazon offers an endless array of products for consumers to buy. When you are a member of the Amazon Associate Program, you have the opportunity to earn income, and if you use these 5 tips, you'll be able to earn plenty of income, so let's have a look.

#1 Choosing a Niche is Key

The very first thing you have to do is decide what your niche will be. In fact, if you don't pick a niche you are destined for failure. This is by far the most important decision you will make. Once you decide on a niche, you can begin to move forward with your money-making agenda.

That's because it is a lot easier to make money through Amazon affiliate program when the people that reach your website or blog are looking for a specific product that your website talks about and then of course also offers the product. When you offer to wide a selection of products, it is more difficult because you don't place as well in the search engines and you don't have the same targeted traffic arriving at your site.

#2 Within Your Content Link to Products

About 50% of income made on Amazon is made through text links placed within the content on the page. Simple text links have proven to be the most effective way to get visitors to click. Web surfers trust the content on web pages more than any other are of a site, and so they are much more likely to click these links than they are to click graphic links.

#3 Product Images Should be Clickable Links

Product images that click through to the affiliate make up about 15% of total Amazon income, and this is relatively easy to do using HTML code.

#4 Create Several Links to Amazon.com

The more links you create to Amazon.com the better. Every link inside your article or content is another opportunity to bring a potential customer to the product and that's an opportunity for you to make a commission. Six to twelve links in an article is perfect.

#5 Highest Conversion on Product Reviews

If you do a high quality product review of the product in your niche you'll get a much higher click thru rate and this means you can increase sales and therefore the amount of commission you earn.

These 5 great tips are a good place to start to generate earnings with Amazon affiliate.

5 Best Kept Secrets to Increased Amazon Affiliate Earnings

Amazon Affiliate Program can generate significant revenue. But it's not always as easy as posting a link and earning money. Here are 5 of the best kept secrets to increase your Amazon Affiliate earnings.

#1 Traffic is Important

Of course, there is more than just the traffic factor, but it is an important one. After all, if you don't have the traffic levels you are not going to make money. Amazon pays between 4% and 8.5% with the average payout being 6%, so you can see that having adequate traffic is important. Consider how you are going to bring this targeted traffic to your site and get them to click through on your Amazon link.

#2 Diversify

It is a good idea not to put all your affiliate efforts into one product. After all, Amazon offers you an endless array of products to choose from. Instead, consider what group of products could be used with your current niche and promote a diversity of products. However, don't spam your blog posts with too many links. Many recommend 6-10 links.

#3 Always be Transparent

Never try to trick your readers to click links they have the potential of paying you a commission. Obviously, you can't label all your affiliate links as such, but you should make some attempt to be transparent. For example, at the end of the blog you could post a disclaimer that your links are associated with the Amazon Affiliate Program (or any other affiliate for that matter). It is all about honesty and your readers want to know that you are being honest and transparent. How that looks on your blog is up to you, but remember just how important it is.

#4 Combine Revenue Streams

Don't be afraid to combine different affiliate programs that will work in your niche. Of course, focusing on your Amazon

Affiliate is important but that does not mean you can't include other affiliates that fit nicely. What you do need to do is read the rules of each of your affiliates. Some do not allow combining so know what the rules are.

#5 Always Track Your Results

Amazon Affiliate Program offers tracking through their statistics software. This is a very important tool to help you know what is selling and what is not. There are other tracking programs. Google Analytics is a popular choice and it's free. Using this type of software will help you be more successful as you'll stop wasting your time on what doesn't work.

There you have it – the five best kept secrets to increasing your Amazon Affiliate earnings.

How to Promote Amazon Affiliate Income

Recently there has been a lot of interest with the Amazon Affiliate Program – that is because it has the potential to generate a comfortable income when done right. But there are some things you should do to improve the likelihood of earning a good income through Amazon.

Don't choose one product to promote, instead choose a set of products that you are going to promote in your niche. For example, let's say your niche is dogs, maybe you could create sub niches – those sub niches could be dog collars, dog leashes, dog beds, dog bowls, dog health care products, dog flea treatments, and the list could go – you get the idea though. Then you need to take the time get to know all about the products in your niche – after all, you will be talking about these products and doing reviews on them. You might be creating top lists and more. When you get to know what you are talking about you will become known as an expert and visitors will continue to come back to see what you have to say about the various products.

Make sure you take the time to create a good landing page on your site. Your landing page needs to sum up everything you have to offer and how it will help your visitors. Your landing page should not be over selling the products you have to offer. If your visitors feel like all you care about is the money, they are not going to have a very positive feel for you. So always create an atmosphere that will build trust. When you do this, your visitors are going to be much more willing to part with their money.

Take the time to focus on your customer in all steps of your transaction. This means from the time your customer first visits your website right through to after sales care. You will create a repeat customer base by treating your customers well and providing the best support you can. It is key to running your business.

As an Amazon affiliate, you have the opportunity to run a very profitable business online. There are numerous people that make a full time income through Amazon and these people get to lead a life that offers them more freedom financially an in their personal lives. They can live the way they want to thanks to their Amazon earnings.

Why You Should Choose Amazon Affiliate Program

There are tons of affiliate programs out there to choose from, but one that gets plenty of focus is the Amazon Affiliate program. Let's look at some reasons why you should consider the Amazon Affiliate program.

1. Amazon is a name you can trust – In fact it's a name that consumers have trusted for a very long time. For you that means more revenue, because they are much more likely to purchase from Amazon, you'll enjoy the benefits in the commissions.

2. Easy to integrate – The number of plugins and tools that integrate with Amazon affiliate continues to grow and that means it is easy for you to integrate your affiliate links into your website or blog.

3. Holidays are gravy – The holiday seasons mean you can make a killing with Amazon affiliate program. It starts in

October and ramps up in December and it is known to be the hottest month on Amazon. Enjoy it.

4. Payment options – Amazon offers affiliates the option of being paid in cash or product. Now that's handy! This means if you want to

5. Amazon is an investment – Think of Amazon like you would any investment. What we mean is that the more time you invest in your Amazon business the more you will reap from it. Increase the number of doorways to the product and you increase the opportunity to generate revenue.

6. Wide selection of products – Amazon has an endless array of products and what that means for you is that you will have no problem finding a niche and then finding products that fit into that niche. You are certainly not limited by the products you have to choose from.

7. Commission increases with sales – The general sales commission is 4 percent, but with just the sale of seven items the commission jumps to 6 percent. That means you can focus on big ticket items but to get to that higher percentage you can sell cheap items. Your commission rate can actually go up to 8.5 percent. Be sure to review the commission schedule on the Amazon site.

8. Adding links is easy – It has never been easier to insert links in your content or articles. It's simply a matter of putting the HTML code in place. It is a simple process that anyone can do, without any special skills or understanding.

Eight simple reasons why you should choose the Amazon affiliate program if you want to make money.

Tips to Improve Earnings With Amazon Affiliate

There's a lot of talk around earning money through the Amazon affiliate program. The amount you earn can vary from a couple hundred to a full time income. Here are some great tips to help you improve your earnings from Amazon affiliate program. Let's have a look.

 *   Build Yourself a Good Email List – Over the years you might have heard this before. It's not new, but it is much easier when you have a website that is focused on selling a physical product compared to digital products. That's because people have their guard up when it comes to digital products like eBooks and how to courses. A great way to get your email list going is to offer something for free. It might be a report on a product, a buyer's guide, etc. Anything that offers the consumer useful information works well. Email lists can be responsible for up to 10 percent of your income. That's a nice chunk.

*   Take Advantage of Holidays with Your Own Promos –
It's pretty common to have thousand dollar days during some of
the main holidays like Cyber Week or Black Friday Week.
While other holidays like Valentines Day or Mother's Day are
less, they are still much higher than the average day, and can be
even higher if you create your own promos. Target every single
holiday to get the most out of holiday revenues. You might do
an article talking about the top 5 products and distribute it for
Black Friday. You might offer a free item for Mother's Day.
You could offer discounts. It's up to you – but don't be afraid to
think outside the box, and do make sure you take advantage of
the opportunity that holidays brings to you.

*   Increase Product Sales to Make More Money – While
this might seem pretty straight forward, the fact is that the
commission rate changes with the more you sell, and that higher
percentage means higher earnings for you. The rate for general
merchandise is 4 percent and can climb to 8 percent with high
sales. During holidays, you can actually reach that 8 percent
with a lot less effort. Selling just 7 items in a month takes you to
a 6 percent commission. Wow! Only 7 items. So you can see
why holidays can be a real benefit to your income.

There you have it – just a few tips to help you improve
your earnings with Amazon affiliate. You too could make a full

time income off the Amazon site like so many others are already doing.

Printed by Libri Plureos GmbH in Hamburg,
Germany

9 786069 837320